Apple books

Apple books

MY FIRST MANDARIN
CHINESE
PHRASES

We study science.
我学习科学.
(wǒ xuéxí kēxué)

May I use your pencil?
我可以用下你的铅笔吗?
(wǒ kěyǐ yòng xià nǐ de qiānbǐ ma)

BY
JILL KALZ

ILLUSTRATED BY
DANIELE FABBRI

TRANSLATOR
TRANSLATIONS.COM

PICTURE WINDOW BOOKS
a capstone imprint

TABLE OF
CONTENTS

HOW TO USE THIS DICTIONARY 3
THE FOUR TONES OF MANDARIN 4
IT SOUNDS LIKE 5

THE BASICS 6
FEELINGS. 8
WHO ARE YOU? 10
MEALS 12
FAMILY 14
DATES AND TIME. 16
MONTHS AND SEASONS 18
WEATHER. 20
SCHOOL. 22
HOME. 24
HOBBIES 26
WITH FRIENDS 28
NUMBERS 30
COLORS 31

READ MORE 32
INTERNET SITES. 32

HOW TO USE THIS DICTIONARY

This book is full of useful phrases in both English and Mandarin Chinese. The English phrase appears first, followed by the Chinese phrase. Look below each Chinese phrase for help to sound it out. Try reading the phrases aloud.

Topic heading in English

Topic heading in Mandarin

Additional phrases to learn

Phrase in English
Phrase in Mandarin
(*Pinyin* pronunciation)

NOTES ABOUT THE MANDARIN CHINESE LANGUAGE

The Chinese language has no alphabet. This language uses characters. Each character stands for an idea or an object. To write a phrase, two or more characters are combined together.

Chinese is the oldest writing system used in the world today. There are thousands of written characters.

In order to write well in Chinese, a person will come to learn up to 4,000 characters.

In this phrase book, the Mandarin characters are shown written in *Pinyin*. *Pinyin* is a system of writing Chinese that spells out the sounds of the words using Roman letters. Most of the *Pinyin* pronunciations can be read like English.

THE FOUR TONES OF
MANDARIN

Chinese is a "tonal" language. By changing the tone of voice, a speaker may change the meaning of a word. For example, the Chinese word "ba" has several meanings.

bā = eight
bá = to pull out
bǎ = target
bà = dad

Pinyin uses four tones. These tones mean that vowel sounds can be said in different ways. To show each of the tones, the *Pinyin* writing uses four accent marks. These accent marks are as follows:

ā, ē, ī, ō, ū = high-level tone, slightly higher than regular speech
á, é, í, ó, ú = rising tone, sound rises like when asking a question
ǎ, ě, ǐ, ǒ, ǔ = dipping tone, sound falls and then rises
à, è, ì, ò, ù = falling tone, starts high and then falls

IT SOUNDS LIKE

Most of the *Pinyin* pronunciations can be read like English. To begin speaking Mandarin, simply sound out each word slowly. The slash mark / shows there are two or more pronunciations for a word. A few *Pinyin* letters have different sounds. You can use this guide to learn how to say these sounds.

	SOUND	PRONUNCIATION	EXAMPLES
CONSONANTS	c	ts	like "its"
	q	ch	like "cheese"
	un	une	like "June"
	x	sh	like "sheep"
	z	dz	like "woods"
	zh	dge	like "fudge"

	SOUND	PRONUNCIATION	EXAMPLES
VOWELS	e	uh	like "cup"
	u	oo	like "broom"
	ü	ew	like "news"

	SOUND	PRONUNCIATION	EXAMPLES
VOWEL COMBINATIONS	ai	ie	like "eye"
	ao	ow	like "cow"
	ei	ay	like "hay"
	ia	ya	like "yacht"
	ou	ow	like "flow"
	ie	ye	like "yell"
	ui	way	like "way"

Mandarin: 基本用语 (jiběn yòngyǔ)

I live in an apartment.
我住在一栋公寓里.
(wǒ zhù zaì yí dòng gōngyù lǐ)

Where do you live?
你住哪里?
(nǐ zhù nǎlǐ)

a house
一座房子
(yí zuò fángzi)

My address is ___.
我的地址是 ___.
(wǒ de dìzhǐ shì ___)

MORE TO LEARN

My phone number is ___.
我的电话号码是 ___.
(wǒ de diànhuà haòmǎ shì ___)
See page 30 for numbers.

Mandarin: 饭 (fàn)

Mandarin: 家庭 (jiātíng)

Do you speak English?
你讲英语吗?
(nǐ jiǎng yīng yǔ ma)

Chinese
汉
(hàny)

French
法
(fǎy)

German
德
(déy)

Spanish
西班牙
(xībānyáy)

A little.
会讲一点.
(huì jiǎng yì diǎn)

MORE TO LEARN

father
爸爸
(bàba)

sister
姐妹
(jiěmèi)

brother
兄弟
(xiōngdc)

Mandarin: 日期和时间 (rìqí hé shíjiān)

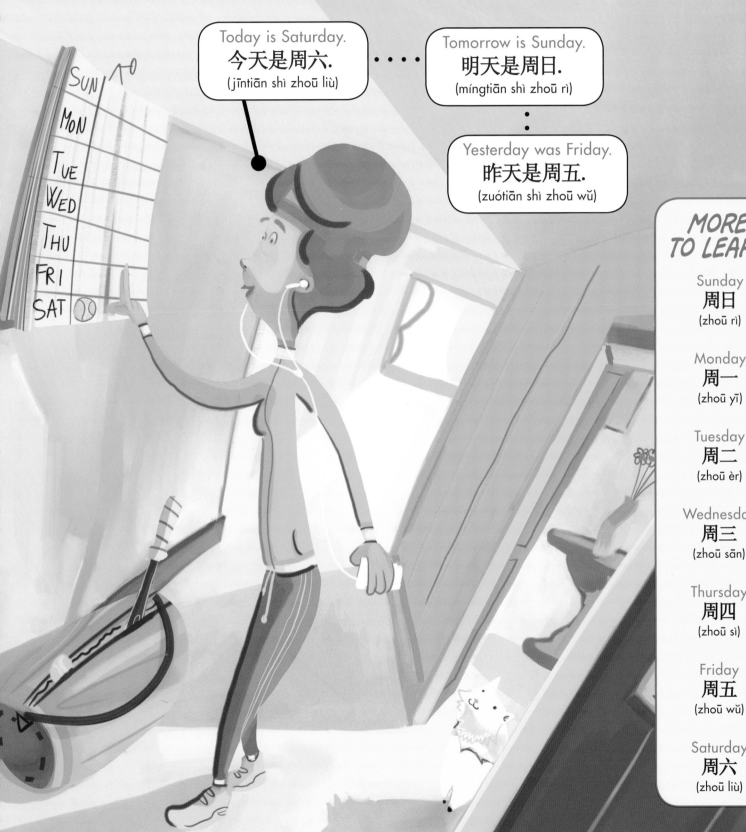

Today is Saturday.
今天是周六.
(jīntiān shì zhōu liù)

Tomorrow is Sunday.
明天是周日.
(míngtiān shì zhōu rì)

Yesterday was Friday.
昨天是周五.
(zuótiān shì zhōu wǔ)

MORE TO LEARN

Sunday
周日
(zhōu rì)

Monday
周一
(zhōu yī)

Tuesday
周二
(zhōu èr)

Wednesday
周三
(zhōu sān)

Thursday
周四
(zhōu sì)

Friday
周五
(zhōu wǔ)

Saturday
周六
(zhōu liù)

Mandarin: 月份和季节 (yuèfèn hé jìjié)

I love summer!
我爱夏天!
(wǒ aì xiàtian)

fall
秋
(qiū)

winter
冬
(dōng)

spring
春
(chūn)

MORE
TO LEARN

January
一月
(yī yuè)

February
二月
(èr yuè)

March
三月
(sān yuè)

April
四月
(sì yuè)

May
五月
(wǔ yuè)

June
六月
(liù yuè)

July
七月
(qī yuè)

August
八月
(bā yuè)

September
九月
(jiǔ yuè)

October
十月
(shí yuè)

November
十一月
(shíyī yuè)

December
十二月
(shier yuè)

It is cold.
冷.
(lěng)

It is hot.
热.
(rè)

It is sunny.
晴天.
(qíng tiān)

Wear a coat.
穿大衣.
(chuān dàyī)

Wear a hat.
戴帽子.
(daì maòzi)

Wear mittens.
戴手套.
(daì shoǔtaò)

Wear boots.
穿靴子.
(chuaṇ xuēzi)

Mandarin: 学校 (xuéxiaò)

Where is the bathroom?
浴室在哪里?
(yùshì zaì nǎ lǐ)

lunchroom
午餐室
(wǔcānshì)

bus stop
车站
(chēzhàn)

Go right.
往右走.
(wǎng yoù zoǔ)

left
左
(zuǒ)

straight ahead
前直
(qián zhí)

Are you ready for the test?
你准备好考试了吗?
(nǐ zhǔnbeì hǎo kaǒshì le ma)

I forgot.
我忘记了.
(wǒ wàngjì le)

23

Where are you?
你在哪里?
(nǐ zài nǎ lǐ)

I am in the kitchen.
我在厨房里.
(wǒ zài chúfáng lǐ)

bathroom
浴室
(yùshì)

bedroom
卧室
(wòshì)

living room
起居室
(qǐjūshì)

dining room
餐室
(cānshì)

Mandarin: 家 (jiā)

What did you say?
你说什么?
(nǐ shuō shénme)

Mom is in the garage.
妈妈在车库里.
(māma zaì chēkù lǐ)

Go outside.
到外面去.
(daò waìmiàn qù)

Go downstairs.
下楼梯.
(xià loútī)

Go upstairs.
上楼梯.
(shàng loútī)

Numbers • 数字 (shùzì)

1 one • 一 (yī)	**11** eleven • 十一 (shíyī)	**30** thirty • 三十 (sānshí)
2 two • 二 (èr)	**12** twelve • 十二 (shíèr)	**40** forty • 四十 (sìshí)
3 three • 三 (sān)	**13** thirteen • 十三 (shísān)	**50** fifty • 五十 (wǔshí)
4 four • 四 (sì)	**14** fourteen • 十四 (shísì)	**60** sixty • 六十 (liùshí)
5 five • 五 (wǔ)	**15** fifteen • 十五 (shíwǔ)	**70** seventy • 七十 (qīshí)
6 six • 六 (liù)	**16** sixteen • 十六 (shíliù)	**80** eighty • 八十 (bāshí)
7 seven • 七 (qī)	**17** seventeen • 十七 (shíqī)	**90** ninety • 九十 (jiǔshí)
8 eight • 八 (bā)	**18** eighteen • 十八 (shíbā)	**100** one hundred • 一百 (yìbǎi)
9 nine • 九 (jiǔ)	**19** nineteen • 十九 (shíjiǔ)	
10 ten • 十 (shí)	**20** twenty • 二十 (èrshí)	

Colors · 颜色 (yánsè)

red · 红色
(hóngsè)

purple · 紫色
(zǐsè)

orange · 橙色
(chéngsè)

pink · 粉色
(fěnsè)

yellow · 黄色
(huángsè)

brown · 棕色
(zōngsè)

green · 绿色
(lǜsè)

black · 黑色
(hēisè)

blue · 蓝色
(lánsè)

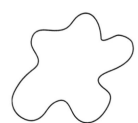
white · 白色
(báisè)

READ MORE

Demarest, **Chris L.** *Mandarin Chinese Picture Dictionary*. Berlitz Kids. Singapore: Bertliz Pub./ APA Publications, 2008.

Kudela, **Katy R.** *My First Book of Mandarin Chinese Words*. Bilingual Picture Dictionaries. Mankato, Minn.: Capstone Press, 2010.

Melling, **David.** *First Chinese Words*. New York: Oxford University Press, 2009.

INTERNET SITES

FactHound offers a safe, fun way to find Internet sites related to this book. All of the sites on FactHound have been researched by our staff.

Here's all you do:

Visit *www.facthound.com*

Type in this code: 9781404871557

 Check out projects, games and lots more at
www.capstonekids.com

LOOK FOR ALL THE BOOKS IN THE SPEAK ANOTHER LANGUAGE! SERIES:

MY FIRST FRENCH *PHRASES*

MY FIRST GERMAN *PHRASES*

MY FIRST MANDARIN CHINESE *PHRASES*

MY FIRST SPANISH *PHRASES*

Editor: Katy Kudela
Designer: Alison Thiele
Art Director: Nathan Gassman
Production Specialist: Danielle Ceminsky
The illustrations in this book were created digitally.

Picture Window Books
1710 Roe Crest Drive
North Mankato, Minnesota 56003
www.capstonepub.com

Library of Congress Cataloging-in-Publication Data
Kalz, Jill.
  My first Mandarin Chinese phrases / by Jill Kalz ; illustrated by Daniele Fabbri.
    p. cm.—(Speak another language)
  Includes bibliographical references.
  Summary: "Simple text paired with themed illustrations invite the reader to learn to speak Mandarin Chinese"—Provided by publisher.
  ISBN 978-1-4048-7155-7 (library binding)
  ISBN 978-1-4048-7246-2 (paperback)
  1. Chinese language—Textbooks for foreign speakers—English—Juvenile literature. 2. Mandarin dialects—Textbooks for foreign speakers—English—Juvenile literature. I. Title.
  PL1129.E5K358 2012
  495.1'83421—dc23   2011027193

Printed in the United States of America in North Mankato, Minnesota.
102011   006405CGS12